I Am

poems by

Tracy Ahrens

Finishing Line Press
Georgetown, Kentucky

I Am

Copyright © 2017 by Tracy Ahrens
ISBN 978-1-63534-251-2 First Edition
All rights reserved under International and Pan-American Copyright Conventions.
No part of this book may be reproduced in any manner whatsoever without written permission from the publisher, except in the case of brief quotations embodied in critical articles and reviews.

Publisher: Leah Maines

Editor: Christen Kincaid

Cover Art: Tracy Ahrens

Author Photo: Tracy Ahrens

Cover Design: Elizabeth Maines McCleavy

Printed in the USA on acid-free paper.
Order online: www.finishinglinepress.com
 also available on amazon.com

Author inquiries and mail orders:
Finishing Line Press
P. O. Box 1626
Georgetown, Kentucky 40324
U. S. A.

Table of Contents

We will be 1
Gesthemane 2
wash me 3
to Michael 4
anam cara 5
all or nothing 6
chasing the sunset 7
these eyes 8
i am 9
light 10
my heart cries 11
desirable, permissible 12
exploration 13
he said 14
i know 15
moon 16
numb 17
retreat 18
stunning 19
the gap 20
the piece 22
possibly 23
Sonnet 24
expected 25
back 26
silent pictures 27
on hold 28

We will be

Words I hear you say.
Talk of one day,
while time endures decay.

Longing, aching, gray;
apart we stay.
Repeated words state "some day."
Emotions in disarray.
Cryptic debt I pay.

Years of temptation play;
neither peace, nor satisfaction stays.

You once drank love each day.
I thirst, crawl, crave;
skin, scent, sounds kept at bay.

"We will be."
Words I hear replay;
teasing me to obey.

Excuses build for your delay;
"would haves" pave this pathway,
then tease me with foreplay,
feeding on our yesterdays.

"We will be."
Training me to stay.
My pain remains downplayed.
Must shred these bonds and break away.

I deserve todays.

Gesthemane

he brought forth spirits—
a fog hovered before us,
moonlight filtered through foamy clouds.

a form stood—still—
to his left,
listening while he spoke.

leaving the listeners,
a light laid under my feet.

cold came quick now,
startling,
a bird shook a bush beside him.

we went to the forest for knowledge and peace,
like Christ to the Garden of Gesthemane.

unknowingly,
they were waiting for him.
he went with no resistance.

i watched,
accepting his fate.

wash me

drops lift layers
of fingerprints,
pores tattooed
by tainted touch.

pale, i pray for
peace, protection,
immunization
from hell's hands.

cleansed and cradled
by divine determination,
God in the gut guides me
this day forward
to righteous arms.

bring him, show me—
faith and hope lead,
to the greatest of these—
called love.

to Michael

In
dreams
forces, firm, pressed
our bodies
together.
Fingers locked, lips
lightly licked
red, blood
flushed our figures
feeling, questioning,
quickly. Crystal eyes
cast to and fro,
our sorrows, smiles
and sins,
from since, until,
and now.
Reality ripped us ripe
from the darkness,
sat us down,
spinning,
slowly—
and stepped away.

anam cara

Friend of my soul
My pulse
My vision

Supporter of quests
My feet
My direction

Acceptor of tears
My heart
My reason

Giver of strength
My muse
My inspiration

Carrier of burdens
My healer
My salvation

all or nothing

It always ends
in the course of one,
if time is needed
the union's done.

Words say friendship
is held so dear,
then sex ends
and all is clear.

It's all or nothing,
accept or blame;
a dive without oxygen,
a winter without flame.

Smiles, confessions,
beliefs now shared;
hearts are opened,
souls are bared.

Then a chord
of truth exhales;
receiver retracts
and feels betrayed.

All or nothing;
no sex, no friend.
A library is stolen,
and that is the end.

chasing the sunset

We chased the light of heaven's eye;
the lids squinted tighter
and tighter
still,
drawing in all the energy of the day.

We stopped to look above us;
sleepy stars stretched,
and smiled,
sprinkling crystal beams that
danced across our faces.

And spinning 'round
we saw the eyelids kiss.

Together we stood and prayed.

Tomorrow we'd chase the light again.

these eyes

what's in these eyes …

 i cannot
place.

they're alive
with
a thousand faces—

and fear.

they stun me—

locking,
testing,
pulling me closer,

like a moth
hovering near flames.

what's in them
seeks freedom,
desires me as a vessel,
to feel,
to learn,
to feast.

i am

a *beautiful* collage of a chaotic life.
stunning truth of loneliness and heartache.
amazing strength against beatings.
talented ways of staying upbeat.
a rare gem, but none protect me.
a *treasure* still undiscovered.
funny, how men run away.
so special no counterpart can be found.
an *angelic* vision that is feared.
a *sexy* form that's never enough.
a *warm* embrace held at arm's length.
uncommonly spiritual amid materialism.
an *oasis* never savored.
a *fascinating* story bound on a shelf.
a *poem* misunderstood.

intelligent enough to flee from the madness.

light

i lost myself helping another,
determined to love,
feeling God;
yet neither speak,
neither are fully understood.
they're mysteries sought,
praised, craved,
yet never fully understood.

tunnel vision,
i saw light;
yet strayed in darkness
until the light extinguished.
no hand reached for me,
no voice whispered,
no clues surfaced as i crawled.

my heart cries

when you're near, or there
my heart cries,
for desire is defeated by reality.

a future seen
is a future ended.
a focus now rests on each day,
a potential need to walk away.
silent:
my heart cries.

if i go, alone,
you will go, too.
going, i'll drag a shadow from my heels.
in your light, that shadow darkens.
intensity—
my heart cries.

images live
even if one more is never made.
a smile strikes often
and my heart cries.

carry me in you
regardless of fate,
forgive me, believe me.

you will go to the earth in me:
the feel, the taste, the scent,
the craving—
along with my heart that cries.

desirable, permissible

what look to give,
a brush against
would cause tribulation.

a touch of hand,
or rest beside
would cause aggravation.

conversation solo,
walking together
would tarnish your reputation.

laughter shared,
a pat on the back
would put you in isolation.

staying near in a crowd,
discussing "next time"
would cause greater separation.

exploration

climbing your shoulder,
my eyes rest on the moon-frosted peak.

in shadows,
hieroglyphics
tell stories of early years.

reading by lunar rays,
my fingers stroke the terrain.

stars draw closer;
winds ride the peak
caressing me in the valley.

many have touched,
have viewed,
have taken

eroding you;
not conquering.

few have stopped
to watch from here,
to discover,
to see.

he said

he said 'I think so'
to a seed of wonder,
inviting in light,
and touch,
and hunger

for love—
sweet words,
songs
and laughter.

he said he's lucky
to have a
girl like me—
to relax,
make love,
travel—

freely.

warm hands
i now remember,
eyes of blue—
that made me surrender

to this lucky
man
seeking love
'ever-after …

i know

hands i remember.
a smile. a laugh.
a sigh while he slept.
beside him i watched.
i laid.
i touched.
his ears,
his hair,
his back.
i know
he felt me
watching,
learning.

moon

i hate you
moon.
always there.
a slice,
whole—
blinding me,
mocking me—
pleasing him,
hurting me.

spin away,
release the sun,
pull in clouds,
bleeding rain.

i hate you
moon.
always there.

numb

lingering pain
turned numb,
lurking in subconscious

forging on,
it's fed by breath,
by light filtered optically.
strong, it beats you,
leaving you lifeless for days.

you pray
for a cure,
believe you've
excised it,

but one sick cell
spreads to a mass
of yesterdays,
dark tomorrows,
empty todays.

retreat

there are times
i feel comfort,
see tomorrows
and nights,
resting,
whole,
studying with touch,
silent
breathing;
and then …

i fear yesterdays,
dark,
voices raising,
secrets,
silence,
accusations,
commanding a divide.

while warm,
i fear attack—
my need to isolate,
retreat,
to turn away.

stunning

knocked senseless
by honesty.
stupefied
by touch.
bewildered
by eyes.
shocked
by candor.
dazed
by thoughts.
confounded
by comfort.
amazed
by loyalty.
astonished
by beauty.
surprised he could feel—

he fled.

the gap

there is comfort
in the gap,
between years
of learning.

what is learned
by looking back,
or ahead?

celestial selection
created this
far-fetched
wonder of

annual hugs
permissible
when planted in
people-packed
settings—

rare scenes,
drawing eyes
that countless
steal for guidance.

royal strength shadows,
protects,
still radiating
the essence of

love,
i know,
none will measure
up to.

what is the fee
for confession,
for private lessons

of chapters
not studied,
of knowledge
he humbly knows?

should one
miss what
never was,
or,
will be?

the piece

where do I fit
in this puzzle
called your life?

a corner?

lost in a field or sea?

jagged, obscure;
where do I belong?

if omitted, could you tell?

others mold around you;
interlocked.
i'm out here in the border,
the last piece before you view the whole.

sorted,
that piece waits,
watches,
knows.

essential, yet overlooked.
uncovered, touched,

passed over for easier moves.

possibly

we lightly touch
our fingers, palms,
a knee across a knee.
a glimpse, a taste
of what could come
or possibly, never be.

while we wait
we register
the pressure, warmth
and feel.
our minds record
each movement,
praying this feeling is real.

Sonnet

A tender thread you weave around us
to spin our souls together mystically;
though pain and tears catch upon its surface,
we weave a patch together faithfully.
A moth, I flew into your cotton sea;
the tempting fiber waves washed o'er my bed
on which you crept and wrapped me instantly
with drowning ecstasy from toe to head.
Morning dew will weigh us down, but instead
of fibers ripping, sticky with the mist,
soft winds swirl around and dry every thread,
freeing our love to live for'er sun-kissed.

In your loving fibers I'll forever
strive to hold our fragile lives together.

expected

readily expected,
unannounced
i'll be rejected.

vanishing touch,
words, feelings,
he'll flee—

words of love
he'll abandon;
making love
he'll abort.

in the end
there is nothing
like there was
at the start.

back

When you leave, do you look
back?
Do you feel
back
holding me so, then saying "I'll be
back
before you know." Time won't hold
back
so you go and I stay
back
longing to know when you'll be
back
so I can hold you and be held—
back.

silent pictures

in silent pictures,
passionate,
we act.

behind my eyes
reels run
images of yesterday.

light enters,
halting vision.

each day frames motions;
distant,
maybe obtainable.

daily,
thoughts pay admission.

on hold

Lifelong
my love has been on hold.

My heart transmitted
through phone lines, ink—
keyboards.

Promises were presented to unite.
Postponed,
I watch for mail,
beat rhythms with lettered keys.
None stimulate sight, touch, smell, taste—
sound of love.

Clicking keys cripple me,
phones are silent,
mail trucks buzz by.

A symphony of sounds scream,
hope accelerates,
ready to spring—
yet restrained.

Reduced, I've rotted.

Distance is the devil.

Tracy Ahrens of Illinois has been a journalist and editor for newspapers, magazines and websites for over 25 years. Currently she is a freelance writer for several publications. Her monthly column on raising her pets can be seen through nine websites and print publications, including: www.tailsinc.com, dogster.com, catster.com, wagthedogUK.com, *American Pet Magazine* and bigbarkonline.com

As of 2017, Tracy had won 60 writing awards statewide, locally and nationally. She is a member of the Illinois Woman's Press Association, National Federation of Press Women, Cat Writers' Association and the Dog Writers Association of America.

For years she's volunteered for animal rescue groups including the Kankakee County Animal Foundation, which she co-founded in 1994. Further, Tracy is an artist, creating graphite pet portraits. Her illustrations have been showcased on note cards for the Kankakee County Animal Foundation in Kankakee, Ill. She's donated portraits for fund-raising events at Anti-Cruelty Society in Chicago, the University of Illinois Wildlife Veterinary Clinic in Champaign-Urbana, Ill.; Critter Corral guinea pig rescue in Steger, Ill.; Hospice Hearts rescue in Champaign-Urbana, Ill. and Crossroads Shih Tzu rescue based in Joliet, Ill. In the past she offered pet portraits through the University of Illinois Small Animal Veterinary Teaching Hospital to help raise funds for their Humane Connection Fund.

Her portrait of a cat titled "Jackson Brown" is on display at the Cat Fanciers' Association Foundation cat museum that opened in June 2011 in Alliance, Ohio. Her portrait of a rabbit named Bosley is on display in the House Rabbit Society's Rabbit Center in Richmond, Calif.

Tracy has written three children's books, *Cloud Jumpers, What if the Moon* and *Sammy Sparrow's First Flight* through Guardian Angel Publishing, and two non-fiction books titled *Giant Hero* (Infinity Publishing) and *Raising My Furry Children*. *Raising My Furry Children* features a guest story by Steve Dale and a portion of the book proceeds is donated to American Brittany Rescue. *Sammy Sparrow's First Flight* is assisting nine humane organizations within the author/artist's hometown area through the sale of each copy. Tracy also published a book of poetry titled *Nature will Heal* by Finishing Line Press (2012).

You can learn more about Tracy at www.tracyahrens.weebly.com

www.ingramcontent.com/pod-product-compliance
Lightning Source LLC
LaVergne TN
LVHW051613080426
835510LV00020B/3279